MARRIAGE

An Essay

By

WILLIAM LYON PHELPS

First published in 1941

British Library Cataloguing-in-Publication Data
A catalogue record for this book is available
from the British Library

CONTENTS

WILLIAM LYON PHELPS

William Lyon Phelps was born on 2nd January 1865, in New Haven, Conneticut, United States.

Phelps earned a B.A. in 1887, writing his thesis on the Idealism of George Berkeley. He then gained an M.A. in 1891 from Yale and his PhD from Harvard in the same year.

During his time a Yale, he offered a course in modern novels which brought the university considerable attention both nationally and internationally. This was quite controversial at the time and Phelps was pressured to give up the course, but eventually, due to popular demand, reinstated it outside the official curriculum.

In 1892, Phelps married Annabel Hubbard, sister of childhood friend Frank Hubbard, and the couple moved to the family estate overlooking Lake Huron. Phelps christened it "The House of the Seven Gables", after the Nathanial Hawthorne story of the same name.

He became a very popular figure at Yale but also as an inspirational orator. He went on lecture tours that drew large audiences, speaking on the virtues of modern literature. He also preached regularly at the Huron City Methodist Episcopal Church and attracted such large crowds that the church was remodelled twice in five years to accommodate them.

Phelps published many essays on modern and European literature, including titles such as *Essays on Modern Novelists* (1910), *Some Makers of American Literature* (1923), and *As I Like it* (1923).

After his retirement from Yale in 1933, after 41 years of service, Phelps continued his public speaking, preaching, and writing a newspaper column. He also sat on book selection committees and acted as a judge for the Pulitzer Prize for literature.

His wife, Annabel, died from a stroke in 1939 and Phelps died four years later, in 1943.

MARRIAGE

DURING FORTY YEARS of teaching college undergraduates, if the lesson for the day was pertinent or an occasion afforded the opportunity, I annually gave one talk to the men in the classroom about their "careers," not concerning vocational training; what I emphasised was the right mental attitude toward life itself, the perhaps inarticulate philosophy underlying choices and ambitions.

I have always been able to speak more intimately to a group of young people than to an individual. The individual must take the initiative. I believe we have no more right to probe into the secret places of the heart than we have to pick a man's pocket. Whenever a student came to me alone and on his own, then I was willing and glad to discuss anything with him. But I believe every man's personality is sacred; an unauthorised or unasked-for attempt to enter it is the worst sort of trespassing.

In the classroom anything may be discussed without embarrassment. No teacher ever had a more intimate class room than mine. For my main interest in literature is its relation to men and women. Browning said his poetry dealt exclusively with the human soul; and it so happens that four poems of Tennyson, which, intentionally or not, are placed together, deal with four terrific passions. The poems are The First Quarrel, Rizpah, The Northern Cobbler, and The Revenge. They deal respectively with Sex, Mother-love, Drinking, and Patriotism. All four have produced happiness and all four have produced murder. Life is dangerous.

Students naturally wish to be successful in their chosen careers. I told them the greatest and most important career was

Marriage. Unlike other careers, Marriage was a career open to every one of them. For among the many and striking differences between male and female, we may observe this: not every woman can be married but every man can. There is always some woman who will marry him.

The highest happiness on earth is in marriage. Every man who is happily married is a successful man even if he has failed in everything else. And every man whose marriage is a failure is not a successful man even if he has succeeded in everything else. The great Russian novelist, Turgenev, said he would give all his fame and all his genius if there were only one woman who cared whether he came home late to dinner. It would have been well if he had known this when he was young.

I told them, "Young gentlemen, although very few of you are now engaged to be married and not one of you is married, your wives are alive; they are living now. You do not know their names or where they are; but isn't it exciting to think that you are every moment drawing nearer to each other? They are half an hour nearer you now than when you entered this classroom. Some in California are asleep for it is not yet dawn; some are eating breakfast in New York; some are eating lunch in Europe. But all your wives are as real as if you were already living with them. What do you intend to do about it?"

Those preparing for the law or medicine will take special studies; those preparing for athletic contests will take special training. If they did not, they would be idiotic. Those who are preparing for marriage should not leave success to chance. For while happiness is sometimes dependent on luck, in the majority of instances it is not. Happiness usually follows proper conditions.

Thus boys and girls, young men and women, will do well if, long before marriage, they train themselves mentally and physically to be successful husbands and wives. It is worth it; for they are in training for the highest prize obtainable on earth, and yet open to and won by millions.

However important sex instruction may be to those about to

be married, there is one thing more important Character. Two people unselfish and considerate, tactful and warm-hearted, and salted with humour, who are in love, have the most essential of all qualifications for a successful marriage-they have Character. People who expect to be married need training in character more than they need instruction in sex.

From childhood boys and girls find out how children come, but the secret of a good character, temperament and disposition is not so readily discovered.

The reason Character is the most important requisite for success in marriage is not merely because it happens to be the chief support of happiness; but those who have character can turn an unsuccessful marriage into a successful one, instead of taking the short way out, and acknowledging failure. No man or no woman is to blame for making a foolish marriage; it might happen to anyone. The test of character is not whether one has or has not made a foolish marriage, the test comes after a foolish marriage has been made. What a triumph then to turn that failure into a success, as the statesman turns a minority into a majority!

I am talking mainly to young people, for those who marry late in life either do not need suggestions or are already incurable. I am in favour of early marriages. I am delighted when either the boy's parents or those of the girl have money enough so that the young pair can be married at twentytwo, before they begin professional study or work. And when there is little money but either or both have a job, they should by all means be married. When young people marry, they take difficulties of housekeeping and privations as a lark, even as young people do camping out. When I was a boy, camping out was absolute bliss. Now it would be absolute horror. Furthermore, in youth neither of them has "set," they can accommodate themselves to each other.

The late President Harper of the University of Chicago was married at nineteen, not so young in his case, for he had already taken his doctor's degree. He told me that during the first five or six years, there were times when neither he nor his wife could

9

write a letter, because they did not have enough cash to buy one postage stamp. He laughed aloud as he recounted this, and added, "There was never one moment when either of us regretted our marriage."

Marriage is a union between masculine strength and feminine loveliness. In the famous play The Barretts of Wimpole Street, Elizabeth exclaimed, "O Robert, how can you love me when you are so strong and I am so weak?" To which came the reply, "Elizabeth, my strength needs your weakness just as much as your weakness needs my strength." Spoken like the man he was. What is the value of being strong unless one can make good use of it? All good qualities grow by exercise.

It takes a great nature to love ardently and faithfully. Shakespeare's ideal soldier is Hotspur, the military hero of King Henry IV. Some of my readers may remember a play by Vicki Baum, called Grand Hotel. A weakling is informed by a physician that he has only a short time to live; whereupon he decides to "make the most of it" and plunges into dissipation. Everyone to his taste; but this is what Hotspur said:

> O gentlemen! the time of life is short
> To spend that shortness basely were too long,
> If life did ride upon a dial's point,
> Still ending at the arrival of an hour.

Toward the close of the first scene of the third act, in the playful laughing dialogue between Hotspur and his wife, we see how happy and intimate was their home life; what perfect understanding existed between them. And he was one hundred per cent masculine.

One more illustration. The finest character in Homer's Iliad was not one of his own countrymen. It was the leader of the enemy. Hector, the Prince of Troy, was the ideal gentleman; if he were alive today, he would be the most popular undergraduate in any American or foreign university. It is said that morals change. They do not. I heard a Chinese scholar deliver an address on Mencius, who "flourished" in the fourth century before Christ. He set forth exactly the qualities that we like to think are characteristics of the best Americans. He upheld courage, modesty, unselfishness, consideration. There never was a time when by decent people these qualities were not considered superior to their opposites. Well, Hector was a shining example of their union in one man, and that man a great soldier, wholly masculine. Toward the close of Book VI of the Iliad Leaf's translation we see how beautiful was his home-life with his wife and little son. He came in the armour of battle to say farewell to both. "So she met him now, and with her went the handmaid bearing in her bosom the tender boy, the little child, Hector's loved son, like unto a beautiful star. . . . So now he smiled and gazed at his boy silently, and Andromache stood by his side weeping, and clasped her hand in his, and spake and called upon his name. Nay, Hector, thou art to me father and lady mother, yea and brother, even as thou art my goodly husband. Come now, have pity and abide here upon the tower, lest thou make thy child an orphan and thy wife a widow."

But Hector, telling her he loved her more than all, said he was the leader of the Trojan forces and must go out to fight. And he added something that makes everyone with sporting blood love him beyond words. He said he knew now that Troy could not win the war; they were all to be destroyed; but his duty was to fight just the same.

And then comes a scene of inexpressible tenderness. As he bent over to kiss the little boy, his son was terrified at the horse-hair plume on his father's helmet. "Then his dear father laughed aloud, and his lady mother." We hear that laughter across thirty centuries. Even in their anguish they laughed aloud, be cause the boy was for a moment afraid of his father. I wonder if a little son today was afraid of his father, would that seem to his parents so incredible?

"Forthwith glorious Hector took the helmet from his head,

and laid it, all gleaming, upon the earth; then kissed he his dear son and dandled him in his arms." Then Hector said what every father for the last million years has said in his heart. He hoped the time would come when men would praise himself, Hector, but that they would say of his son, "Far greater is he than his father." Every normal father has longed to have his son become greater than he. Once a year I used to tell this Homeric story to my undergraduates and say, "Remember! you are carrying the family flag; at home there are those who hope that you will bring the greatest honour to the family name, far surpassing all who have gone before."

Marriage can be wonderful from every point of view, when it is a combination of the highest physical delight with the highest spiritual development. It is indeed the sublimation of the senses. The great novelist, George Meredith, who hated priggishness in all its forms, said in a letter, "I have written always with the perception that there is no life but of the spirit; that the concrete is really the shadowy; yet that the way to spiritual life lies in the complete unfolding of the creature, not in the nipping of his passions. An outrage to Nature helps to extinguish his light. To the flourishing of the spirit, then, through the healthy exercise of the senses."

Could there be a better description of the union of physical and spiritual development in marriage than his phrase The complete unfolding of the creature?

To his son Meredith wrote, "Look for the truth in everything, and follow it, and you will then be living justly before God. Let nothing flout your sense of a Supreme Being, and be certain that your understanding wavers whenever you chance to doubt that he leads to good. We grow to good as surely as the plant grows to the light.... Do not lose the habit of praying to the unseen Divinity. Prayer for worldly goods is worse than fruitless, but prayer for strength of soul is that passion of the soul which catches the gift it seeks."

What is love? Boys and girls fall in love at about the age of six or seven, and often while growing up, with a good many different persons. I say they fall in love for one does not have to explain to them what romantic love means. They have the symptoms described in the mediaeval romances, in novels, in love-poems, in sentimental songs.

But this is not exactly the same thing as married love which grows by companionship and by sharing sorrows as well as pleasures. Many years ago a college friend of mine, a splendid fellow with everything to make life worth living, was married to a fine girl. He died during the first weeks of the honeymoon. I said to a man of sixty, "Can anything be more tragic than that?" "Yes," he replied unhesitatingly, "it is more tragic when the husband or wife dies after twenty-five years of marriage."

He was accurate both ways; the loss after twenty-five years is more terrible; and in the instance I mentioned the shattered and desolated bride was in two years happily married to a second husband, which was right and wise.

The overwhelming passion of love is certainly rapture and marriage is its most satisfying consummation. But true love is not so expressive in desire for possession as it is in consideration for the welfare of the beloved object. "Oh, how I love you! " may not mean as much as "Don't go out without your rubbers on." Do you remember that passage in Guy de Maupassant where the husband said just that to his wife? And they were astounded when the maiden aunt who had lived with them for years without a word of dissatisfaction, who had gone in and out of the room as unremarked as the family cat, who was thought to be incapable of emotion, suddenly burst into a storm of weeping and cried, "No one has ever cared whether or not I had my rubbers on 1 "

Do you remember Browning's poem Muleykeh where the owner allowed his favourite mare, the Pearl, to be stolen when he could have overtaken her on an inferior horse, and his friends said he was a fool? He replied sobbing, "But she would have been beaten in speed You never have loved m y Pearl."

Is it love to dishonour a woman? Isn't it greed?

Yet expressions of love and passion, embraces and caresses, are also essential. I told my students, "After you are married, never leave the house, even if only to post a letter at the corner, without kissing your wife." This very simple act is an important preservative of married happiness.

I also advised them during the first twenty years of marriage to occupy the same bedroom. Quarrels and even insults given in the heat of anger are certain to happen in nine marriages out of ten. It is supremely important not to let these flames of resentment become a fatal conflagration. They must not last.

> And blessings on the falling out,
> Which all the more endears,
> When we fall out with those we love,
> And kiss again with tears!

Although happy marriages are common unhappy ones are still news), the only ideal, flawless marriages I ever heard of were those of the Brownings and the Hawthornes; in both instances the husbands were men of genius and the wives almost angelic.

Since the greatest of all the arts is the art of living together and since the highest and most permanent happiness depends on it, and since the way to practice this art successfully lies through character, the supreme question is how to obtain character.

The surest way is through Religion -Religion in the Home. All that we know for certain of every person is that he is imperfect. Human imperfection means a chronic need for improvement. The most tremendous and continuous elevating, purifying, strengthening force is Religious Faith.

My parents neglected my social training. I am sorry they did. They were careless about my clothes and my personal appearance. I am sorry for it. But I am constantly grateful for their religious and spiritual training. Every day of my life I am grateful. They knew it was more important than anything else in the world.

I was taken to church before I could walk; and as soon as I

could walk I walked to church twice every Sunday, to church and Sunday School in the morning, to church again in the evening. My father asked a blessing on every meal, and conducted family prayers morning and evening. I began to read the Bible through when I was five years old. My father and mother read the Bible every day of their lives. I was brought up on Bible phrases; they were the stuff and substance of daily conversation.

I was baptized and joined the church when I was eleven; I have been a regular and active church-member ever since. I would rather belong to the church than belong to any other organisation or society or club. I would rather be a church-member than receive any honour or decoration in the world.

On a certain occasion, Ralph Waldo Emerson dropped in on a Sunday morning at a little country village church. It was only sparsely occupied, the people did not look brilliant, and the preacher was rather dull. At first he felt something akin to contempt for this apparently commonplace group. Suddenly it came over him that these people were assembled exclusively for the most important purpose that can inspire the human mind- the individual's personal relation to Almighty God. Then the little church and the little group took on an air of the sublime.

It amuses me when I read novels written by those who never had any religious faith or have lost it, novels that describe religious training in the home as producing unhappiness and hypocrisy and morbidity, with an atmosphere of thick gloom. As I look back on my childhood, it seems to me that the house was full of laughter. Table conversation was enlivened with mirth. If there ever was a merry household, it was ours. Our daily existence was full of fun, and Christmas, New Year's, Fourth of July, and birthdays were delirious.

This is normal and natural and logical. Religious faith is a central heating plant, it warms and energises one's whole existence. It gives a reason for life itself, for development. It gives a philosophy for conduct, and far more important, it emotionalises conduct, even more strongly than athletics and patriotism.

I am often called an optimist, and I suppose I am, because I believe that eventually Truth will conquer Error and Good conquer Evil. But I am not such an optimist as those who have no religious faith, who believe there is no future life, who believe there is no mind, no soul, no personality, only animal functions, and who yet are cheerful. I do not blame them for a loss of religious faith or of faith in survival, for everyone should believe what seems to him to be true; but to believe that human beings, whose minds are adapted for eternal development as the fish is adapted for water, yet have exactly the same fate as grasshoppers, and to remain cheerful under this assumption, requires an optimism that infinitely surpasses Pollyanna.

After listening once to a learned scientist delivering a lecture in which he used his brilliant mind to prove that he had no mind, I asked one who shared his belief, "I understand why you say all this; but why do you seem to enjoy it?"

"Ah," he replied, "we have such good times making our experiments." Exactly; exactly the way a child enjoys making mud pies, and with equal significance.

No, I rather admire the position taken by Edna St. Vincent Millay, who if I understand her correctly, has no religion. She wrote a poem about the death of those who are young and fair, and wrote with the defiance of despair. These things are so; but I will not be reconciled!

I admire the absolute pessimism of the great poet, A. E. Housman, who called himself an atheist, because he thought it was impossible that any god could be so utterly base as to create marvellous minds for a contemptible life and destiny.

Of all essential things, the most essential in married life and in the bringing up of children is Religion. When two people are engaged and are making plans for living together, they are sure to discuss religion. You remember how, suddenly Margaret turned to Faust and asked him point-blank, "Do you believe in God? Glaubst du an Gott?"

A chief reason why bringing up children is so difficult an

art is that example is so much more important than precept. I am a qualified literary critic, although I never wrote a novel; I am a qualified drama critic, although I never wrote a play; I am a qualified baseball and lawn tennis critic, although I never was a first-class player. But when parents endeavour to bring up children to reflect honour on the family and to be useful members of society, the parents

must set a good example. Emerson said, "What you are thunders so loud I cannot hear what you say."

A man once wrote to Carlyle asking him if he ought to teach his little children to say their prayers. The austere Scot replied, "Yes, but only if you pray yourself. Don't teach them anything in which you yourself do not believe."

The Scot was right. To teach little children to say their prayers when the parents never say them themselves is like teaching a dog to say his prayers, a trick that seems to amuse many people. To have little children say grace at the table when no adult in the room has any faith is again only a pretty trick. But to send them to church when the parents stay away is far worse; it is culpable. Then the children regard church-going, praying, and religion as some of the innumerable burdens and penalties of childhood, from which they will escape as soon as they reach independence.

When Johnny Overton, the great Yale athlete, who was killed in the war, left his Tennessee home to go to college, his father told him that he would not give him any advice as to his morals or behaviour; "but, Johnny, will you promise me that you will never go to sleep at night until you have said your prayers?" John promised; and afterwards told his father he had kept his word.

If both young husband and wife share a similar religious belief, it is an enormous asset; an immense help to permanence in married happiness. Now one cannot believe in God and in Our Lord merely by wishing to do so. Yet I often think that many who do not believe do not really wish to with passionate earnestness; with as strong a wish as they have for money or for good looks or for popularity.

There are many who say and more who think without saying, "If I only had the faith I had as a child! Then I believed in God and in Jesus Christ and in heaven."

One might almost as well say, "if I only had the knowledge of algebra I had as a child!" Why do small boys and girls know algebra and why in later years do they not know it? Because when they were at school they gave their attention to it; they studied it; they thought about it. But thirty years have passed without their once opening the book or considering the subject.

I met a woman whom I had not seen since she was eighteen; and I asked her to play the piano. "Oh, I can't!" "But you used to play beautifully." "Yes, but I haven't touched the keys since I was married."

What does one expect? If one experiences regret for the lost faith of childhood, it is proper to ask, "How long is it since you read the Gospels? How long is it since you prayed?"

Since religious faith is such an asset to happiness, such a foundation for character and for married life and bringing up children, one might make an effort to recover it or at least to consider it.

I believe Sunday should be a day of joy and happiness; Sunday afternoon games and recreation are fine; but one enjoys them more if one has been to church in the morning or spent part of the day in either solitary or community worship. Those parents who selfishly seek only their own pleasures every week end, and who do nothing but amuse themselves, are they likely to bring up their children successfully?

To those who have no faith and to those who have lost it, let me recommend some wise words by Dean Inge.

There are those who are as explosively and suddenly "converted" as was St. Paul; but there are also those who cannot have such an experience; and many, many are the ways to God. One should give the matter serious attention; it deserves it. It is the most serious of all things.

Being educated means to prefer the best not only to the worst but to the second best. It means in music to prefer Beethoven not only to jazz but to Brahms. So it is in all forms of art, in athletics, in politics, in everything.

Now the Person celebrated in the Gospels is the greatest Personality in history. He knew more about life than Shakespeare. He was the greatest nerve specialist who ever lived. "Come unto me, . . . and you shall find rest unto your souls." His way is incomparably the best way; it is the way to peace of mind, to courage, independence, fearlessness, to joy. If we find faith lacking, try His way.

Listen to Dean Inge: he is discussing the illumination of the mind that follows recognition o f the Master. "Religious life begins with Faith, which has been defined ... as the resolution to stand or fall by the noblest hypothesis. This venture of the will and conscience progressively verifies itself as we progress on the upward path. That which began as an experiment ends as an experience. We become accustomed to breathe the atmosphere of the spiritual world."

If one follows the prescription of a physician and finds it beneficial, one believes in the physician.

Young people about to be married, young people recently married, young fathers and mothers should give Religion the most serious consideration. To neglect it, to be indifferent to it, is worse and more foolish than to be antagonistic. Religion is not a frill or an ornament or a luxury; still less is it a thing to clutch at only in danger or in heartbreak.

Religion is the greatest creative force in the world; it has made thousands of saints and thousands of heroes; it has revolutionised innumerable individual lives. It has changed people from selfishness to unselfishness; from cowardice to courage; from despair to hope; from vulgarity to decency; from barrenness of life to fruitfulness.

Religious faith has produced the finest architecture, the finest painting, the finest music, the finest literature in the world. When Religion can change the lives of millions, when it can produce supreme creations in art, it is a force worth serious consideration.

The late John Philip Sousa, the famous composer and bandmaster, said that the reason why there was not so much great music produced in the twentieth as in the nineteenth century, was because religious faith had declined. According to him, creation is based on faith. This may be claiming too much, but his testimony as a composer is interesting.

Religion is not a dream or an illusion or a phantasy. I saw a quotation from Doctor Jung's book, Psychology and Religion, which runs as follows: "Religious experience is absolute and indisputable and must signify something related to the archetype or unconscious mental background of all of us." In this sentence the word archetype means an objective Reality, like a Model of which individual examples are imitations.

The American philosopher, Paul Elmet More, who died in 1937, and who was one of the most profound scholars in the world, after prolonged thought and study and observation, came from agnosticism into a complete and passionate faith in the Christian religion and in the Incarnation. He said that while Love was the main principle in religion as a way of life, the most important contribution to humanity made by religion was Hope. Hope in the destiny of man, in the superlative value of the individual, in the personality of our Father in Heaven.

I might add that if hope deferred maketh the heart sick, hope destroyed maketh the heart dead.

The very last word to describe religious faith is the word anesthetic. Religious faith is a comfort to the old, the sick, and the suffering; but in general it is not a sedative, it is a tonic. It is a dynamo; it is a driving force. Henry Drummond, the most effective speaker on religion I can remember, said to a group of students, "I ask you to become Christians not because you may die tonight, but because you are going to live tomorrow. I come not to save your souls, but to save your lives."

Lord Charnwood, the famous biographer of Lincoln, a scholar and a business man, said he took up the Gospel of St. John, and

as a professional writer of biography, studied it impartially. The result was, "I found myself at the end
just an ordinary Christian." And he wrote a book called According to St. John.

Religion adds an enormous zest to daily life; it makes everything interesting and significant. It keeps alive the capacity of wonder. I myself am interested in everything in the world, from a sandlot ball game to the nebula in Orion. But the mainspring of my existence, the foundation of my happy and exciting life, is Christian faith.

I suggest to those recently married and those about to be married that they are entering into a relationship that can bring them the highest and most lasting happiness or the most crushing disillusion and despair. Such a relationship is particularly remarkable because of its intimacy, an intimacy far transcending that of friendship, love of parents or any earthly emotion. As Thomas Hardy said, Marriage annihilates reserve. In this amazing intimacy, every care should be taken to ensure success. A common interest in religion, saying prayers together, will help enormously toward increasing and preserving happiness.

For a true belief in the Christian religion will improve daily manners. Husband and wife will not take each other for granted; they will not become stodgy or commonplace or stereotyped. The man will not use the newspaper at the breakfast table as a screen. Bad table manners have caused many divorces.

Tennyson has given us in The Princess the real kind of marriage which one of my students described in the vernacular. He wrote to me, "I am going to be married. It won't be much of a wedding, but it will be a wonderful marriage."

Listen to Tennyson:
For woman is not undevelopt man,
But diverse: could we make her as the man,
Sweet Love were slain: his dearest bond is this,
Not like to like, but like in difference.

Yet in the long years liker must they grow;
The man be more of woman, she of man:
He gain in sweetness and in moral height,
Nor lose the wrestling thews that throw the world;
She mental breadth, nor fail in childward care,
Nor lose the childlike in the larger mind;
Till at the last she set herself to man,
Like perfect music unto noble words.

A wife may be a civilising force; that is well; but she may be far more than that. She may be a revelation in daily intimacy more unconsciously impressive than a professional saint.

This is what Caponsacchi said of an imagined union with Pompilia:

To live, and see her learn, and learn by her,
Out of the low obscure and petty world
Or only see one purpose and one will
Evolve themselves i' the world, change wrong to right;
To have to do with nothing but the true,
The good, the eternal-and these, not alone In the main
current of the general life,
But small experiences of every day,
Concerns of the particular hearth and home:
To learn not only by a comet's rush
But a rose's birth, -not by the grandeur,
God, But the comfort, Christ.